DISASTER!
DROUGHTS

By Dennis Brindell Fradin

Consultant:
Donald T. Jensen, Ph. D.
Certified Consulting Meteorologist
Denver, Colorado

 CHILDRENS PRESS, CHICAGO

*Drying, cracked
mud of the South
Dakota Badlands*

Library of Congress Cataloging in Publication Data

Fradin, Dennis B.
  Droughts.

  (Disaster!)
  Includes index.
  Summary: Discusses the causes and effects of drought,
including the dust storms that devastated the Great
Plains during the 1930s and other periods of
disastrous drought and famine throughout history.
    1. Droughts—Juvenile literature. [1. Droughts.
  2. Rain and rainfall. 3. Water supply. 4. Disasters]
  I. Title. II. Series: Fradin, Dennis B. Disaster!
  QC929.D8F73 1983   551.57'73   83-10073
  ISBN 0-516-00858-7   AACR2

TABLE OF CONTENTS

The Great Plains settlers of the 1800s were called "sodbusters" because the grass-covered ground was so tough to break up (below). Trees were so scarce on the Great Plains that many settlers built houses of sod (above) instead of wood.

1/THE "DIRTY THIRTIES"

During the late 1800s, settlers poured into the Great Plains of the United States. Families piled into wagons and followed trails that led to Nebraska, Kansas, Texas, and Oklahoma. They built homes and began to farm and ranch.

Before planting their seeds, the farmers had to plow the ground. Plowing was difficult on the Great Plains. The prairie grasses held the dirt together like glue. The sod (grass-covered ground) was so tough to break up that the settlers of the 1800s were nicknamed "sodbusters." Once the grasses were dug up and the ground was turned, the farmers planted corn or wheat and hoped for rain.

The Great Plains ranchers didn't have to dig up the sod. They let their cattle and sheep graze on the rich grasses. After the livestock ate away the natural vegetation in one place, the ranchers would move their livestock to new grazing grounds.

Because of this continual plowing and grazing, the Great Plains had less and less grassland every year. The farmers and herders knew very little about soil conservation. They didn't realize that by destroying the native grasses and not replanting them, they were removing the "glue" that held down the soil.

The settlers didn't really have time to worry about the soil. Most had trouble just surviving. During times of little rain—called *droughts*—crops withered and died. From time to time, huge swarms of grasshoppers ate the crops. Winter blizzards killed livestock by the thousands.

Faced with these hardships, some farmers and ranchers gave up and returned East. But many stayed and turned the Great Plains into the nation's major food-producing center.

The demand for Great Plains crops reached a new high during World War I (1914-18). American soldiers needed food. Wheat grown on the Great Plains was sold at high prices and then made into bread. "Plant more wheat—it'll help us win the war!" Americans proclaimed.

Young wheat held down the soil only one thirtieth as well as the native grasses had done. But there was a war to be won, so millions of acres of the unfarmed grasslands were plowed away. Golden wheat grew high over long stretches of Kansas, Nebraska, Colorado, Oklahoma, and Texas.

The good times for the farmers and ranchers continued after World War I. The battered European nations were badly in need of food. The Great Plains, which were producing corn and cattle in addition to wheat, became known as one of the richest food-producing regions of the world.

Even the weather seemed to be on the side of agriculture. Beginning in about 1910 and continuing for twenty years, the middle of the United States received ample rainfall.

But bad weather brought an end to this period of prosperity. The year 1930 was dry in the United States. Crops withered in many states. Droughts struck again in 1931. The 1930s was a decade of prolonged, terrible droughts. In fact, between 1930 and 1936, Vermont and Maine were the only states in the country that escaped drought.

If you've ever seen grass turn brown and die after it's gone a long time without water, you know what happens in a drought. During the droughts of the 1930s, farmers watched helplessly while their wheat, corn, and other crops withered and died. In many places, the dry, cracked land looked as though a giant dragon had breathed fire across the countryside.

With few crops and no native grasses anchoring the soil, the

The droughts and dust storms of the 1930s left desolate farms (left) and sand-covered Santa Fe railroad tracks (above) in Oklahoma. Today, the Santa Fe runs through lush, green countryside (below).

The "black blizzard" dust storms of the 1930s, like this one in Liberal, Kansas (right), made it necessary for people outdoors to cover their faces with dust masks to avoid choking (above).

8

Great Plains were like a giant, dry baseball infield. When winds swept through the region, the loose dirt and sand were picked up and whirled over hundreds of square miles of land. The era of *dust storms* began.

One of the first major dust storms of the 1930s struck on May 9, 1934. On that day, wind kicked up millions of tons of dirt from Montana and Wyoming and sent it flying eastward. In Wisconsin, drifts of dust piled up on fields like brown snow. This dust storm blew across Massachusetts, New York, and other eastern states. Dust from Montana and Wyoming even dropped on ships in the Atlantic Ocean.

People called the dust storms of the 1930s *black blizzards.* During black blizzards, people outdoors had to cover their faces to avoid choking, and grope their way home. The whirling dirt could blot out the sunlight.

Judy Marrett, who lived in Grand Island, Nebraska during the 1930s, recalls trying to drive during black blizzards: "I can remember driving from Scottsbluff, Nebraska to another town in Nebraska. We had to keep the car lights on to see the road because it was so dark from blowing dust. This was in the middle of the afternoon."

Inside homes, people covered their windows and doorways with wet cloths when they saw the black clouds coming. But dust found its way through even the tiniest cracks. The dust settled on people's food at dinnertime, landed in their mouths while they slept, and piled up around their houses.

To avoid breathing dust, many persons kept masks handy. Yet dozens of people—it is not known exactly how many—died from breathing too much dust. For as long as four days at a time, the dust storms forced businesses to close, blew paint off cars and homes, and carried away precious topsoil from farmlands.

Above: It was so dark during this 1935 dust storm in Dodge City, Kansas that people in cars had to turn their lights on to be able to see. Below: Dodge City today.

Above: A farmer and his sons struggle through a 1936 Oklahoma dust storm. Previous dust storms had completely covered this farmland with drifting soil and sand.
Below: Because of conservation efforts since the droughts and dust storms of the 1930s, the earth of the Great Plains can now hold the rain it needs and crops can grow.

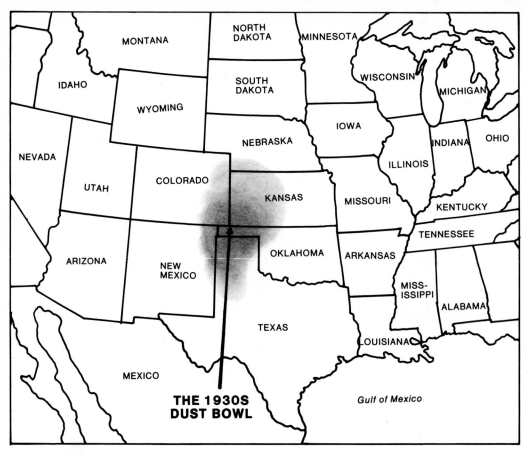

THE 1930S DUST BOWL

Because the United States and Canada experienced hundreds of dust storms during the 1930s, that decade is sometimes called the "Dirty Thirties." Although black blizzards blew through much of North America, one area suffered many of the worst storms. Known as the "Dust Bowl," this region included parts of Kansas, Colorado, New Mexico, Texas, and Oklahoma.

Virgie Mathews grew up in Kerrick, Texas, and moved to Griggs, Oklahoma when she got married. She remembers what it was like to live in the Dust Bowl: "The really black dust storms usually came from the north. At first we'd see them way off on the horizon and they'd look like big storms coming up. When they got here they'd be rolling and full of turmoil and really dangerous looking. I remember one in particular that was so black you couldn't see in it at all."

By now, Americans realized that droughts were only partly to blame for the black blizzards. People were equally to

12

This pile of poisoned grasshoppers in Pierre, South Dakota was raked up off a small lawn, but not before the insects had eaten the bark and leaves of the trees and destroyed the crops.

blame. By stripping the ground of its natural grasses, farmers and ranchers had removed the topsoil's natural glue. This made it easy for the wind to lift up the dirt.

Another horror accompanied the droughts—grasshoppers. Hot, dry weather is perfect for hatching grasshoppers, and the young insects can eat away whole fields of crops. From 1934 to 1938, grasshoppers destroyed over $315 million in crops. Poisons were used to kill the insects, but the grasshoppers were as much trouble dead as alive. In places, dead grasshoppers made pavements so slippery that cars skidded off roads.

Along with the grasshoppers, hungry rabbits also devoured crops. Groups of farmers clubbed the rabbits to death. Because food was scarce, people often ate the rabbit meat.

The droughts, dust storms, and grasshopper attacks of the 1930s came at a bad time. The United States was in the midst of the Great Depression. Millions of people were out of work in the cities. Because of drought, conditions were terrible for millions of farm people, too.

Thousands of poverty-stricken families from the Dust Bowl packed up and headed west when they could no longer eke out a living from their land. This family had gotten as far as Tracy, California when their car broke down.

There was so much poverty in and around the Dust Bowl that many families packed up and left. During the 1930s Oklahoma's population dropped by sixty thousand. In all, hundreds of thousands of persons left the Great Plains during the 1930s.

Most of these "Okies," as they were called, headed for the West Coast, particularly California. Those who were lucky found low-paying jobs out West. Thousands who had no money lived in "tent cities" or even in their cars.

The federal government helped those who remained on their farms by arranging loans and by paying a guaranteed price for a certain portion of their crops. The government also tried to prevent more dust storms by giving money to farmers who let part of their land remain in grass. Rain in the late 1930s and early 1940s also helped the farmers recover.

The Dust Bowl era taught an important lesson: a new outlook toward managing the land was needed. Scientists knew that future droughts couldn't be prevented—droughts are a regular part of nature. But they hoped to prepare people for droughts and limit the damage done by poor rainfall.

This windbreak, planted in 1944, helps block the Great Plains winds.

Beginning in the 1930s scientists, government officials, and farmers began to work together on drought problems. Dams and canals were built to bring irrigation water to dry farmlands. Farmers learned how to make better use of limited rainfall. Trees were planted to help block the Great Plains winds and to cool the air. In addition, laws were passed to keep a certain amount of land covered by natural vegetation.

Droughts and dust storms did return to the United States. In 1954, a black blizzard filled the sky with dust from the Canadian border to Amarillo, Texas. As eighty-mile-an-hour winds blew dust four miles into the sky, cattle choked to death, businesses closed, and people were stranded in cars. The dust storms during the 1950s were so bad that many people called the decade the "Filthy Fifties."

In the 1970s droughts and dust storms hit California and other Western states. Herds of cattle died, and farmers had to cover their faces with ski masks as they plowed the land.

These storms caused serious problems, but because people had learned more about taking care of the land, the damage never equaled the devastation of the Dirty Thirties.

During the years of drought and dust storms, tons of dust and sand ruined farms
that had been worked since the late nineteenth century. These farms in
Guymon, Oklahoma were only a few miles from the Everett farm in Stratford, Texas.

2/"DIRTY THIRTIES" SURVIVORS

What is it like to see your fields parched by droughts? What is it like to have thick dust blown into your home, or to see millions of grasshoppers devouring your crops? How does it feel to lose a farm you have worked so hard to save? There are many people living today who had these experiences during the "Dirty Thirties."

R. K. and Winnie Everett-Stratford, Texas

R.K. and Winnie Everett, both born and raised in Texas, were married in 1921. They settled on a farm a few miles south of Stratford, Texas. The Everetts grew wheat and maize and raised cattle.

"About 1931 the Dust Bowl days started," remembers R.K. Everett, now eighty-four years old. "It was dry from about 1931 to about 1937, and we didn't raise much to speak of except weeds.

"We planted seeds—the government gave us seed loans for about five years—but they didn't grow. It showered now and then, but there just wasn't enough rain. Today the farmers around here get irrigation water from wells, but we didn't have that back then. The crops we grew during the drought weren't even worth harvesting. It stayed dry so long we had to give up our cattle because there wasn't enough for them to eat.

"Fortunately we were able to keep our farm. It was kind of scarce sometimes, but we managed."

Winnie Everett, R.K.'s wife of more than sixty years,

remembers the dust storms that struck Stratford, which was in the heart of the Dust Bowl. "We taped our windows and tried most everything to keep the dust out, but we couldn't. You know that stuff they clean your teeth with? That's what the dust tasted like. There were times it got so dark from the dust storms we went to meet our kids at school to bring them home."

In spite of these circumstances, says Winnie Everett, "I don't just remember the hard times. I remember the loving part, too. People knew their neighbors better then because everyone was sharing hard times. Neighbors would come to each other's houses. We'd play cards or go outside and play horseshoes if it wasn't too dusty. People helped their neighbors who were in need. The Dust Bowl days often brought out the best in people that way."

June Rachuy Brindel and Her Sisters, Judy Marrett and Bessie Peters

The youngest of seven children, June Rachuy Brindel was born on a farm in Little Rock, Iowa in 1919. When she was still a child, a depression struck Iowa and her father lost his farm. During the summers, June stayed with older brothers and sisters in Iowa, South Dakota, and Nebraska. She saw how drought affected her family in these states.

These cars are making their way through an Iowa dust storm.

Above left: George and Judy Marrett
Left: Bessie Rachuy Peters
Above: June Rachuy Brindel

"Although my dad had lost his Iowa farm, he still owned one in South Dakota," Mrs. Brindel recalls fifty years later. "My oldest brother and his wife went out to South Dakota to try to grow enough to keep the farm going." Ten-year-old June spent the summer of 1929 at the South Dakota farm, which had already been hit by drought.

"There were very few trees around the South Dakota farm, and the wind just kept blowing. Dust blew all the time. The crops simply would not grow. I remember the wild pheasants got so hungry that they came right up to the house looking for food. My brother would come and grab them and we'd have pheasant for dinner. It was survival of the fittest."

19

Soil had drifted over this South Dakota farm building in 1935.

Because of the drought, the South Dakota farm could not pay for itself. Like the family farm in Little Rock, Iowa, it, too, was lost.

In 1935, when she was sixteen years old, June spent the summer with her sister Judy in Grand Island, Nebraska. "There was really, really a drought in Nebraska—everyone was talking about it," June remembers.

"We'd picnic right in the middle of the bed of the Platte River," adds June's sister, Judy Marrett. "There was absolutely not one drop of water in it. The kids would dig in the sand, and they'd have to go a foot down or more before finding a wet spot."

"There were dust storms in Nebraska all the time," continues June. "My sister Judy would put wet bath towels on the windowsills to keep the dust out, but it would come in through the cracks and get all over everything. When you'd go outside you had to hold a handkerchief over your nose. I was young and healthy, but I'm sure there were people with lung ailments who died because of all the dust in the air."

Thousands of grasshoppers gathered on this house in Pierre, South Dakota. These ravenous insects not only ate farm crops and entire gardens, in places they also ate the paint off buildings.

Mrs. Brindel has one particularly nightmarish memory of Nebraska. "Once we thought we saw a dark cloud in the west and people got excited because they thought it was a rain cloud. It was no rain cloud. It was grasshoppers—millions of them. They batted against the windows and got squashed. When we went back outside we saw thousands of dead grasshoppers on the ground. The garden was gone. The grasshoppers had eaten it up."

During the 1930s June also spent several summers with her sister Bessie Peters, who lived on a farm in Gilmore City, Iowa. Bessie and her husband grew corn, oats, flax, and barley and raised milk cows, pigs, and chickens. Drought destroyed their crops and killed the pasture grasses.

Bessie Peters still remembers the terrible dust storms in Gilmore City. "You know how ditches fill with snow in winter? They'd fill the same way in summer, only it would be with dirt and dust. Fence posts in places were covered by dust, too. We lost a lot of topsoil from our farm and so did everyone else. I suppose a lot of the best soil wound up in the Mississippi River and the Gulf of Mexico."

From out in space, most of the earth's surface looks blue (right) because more than 70 percent of the planet's surface is water. The largest body of water on earth is the Pacific Ocean (below).

3/DROUGHTS: WHAT, WHERE, WHY, AND HOW

From out in space, the planet Earth looks like a blue, green, and white jewel. Forests and farms create the green. The white is from clouds, snow, and ice. But most of Earth's surface looks blue because more than 70 percent of our planet's surface is water—oceans, rivers, lakes, and ponds.

It is fortunate that the earth has so much water. Every plant and animal needs water to survive. A potato is about 80 percent water and a tomato is about 95 percent water. About two thirds of your body is made of water.

Earth's Water

There is always the same amount of water on earth. No new water is made, and none ever disappears. Water you washed your hands with today may have been bathwater for George Washington two hundred years ago. Water in your backyard mud puddle may have been drunk by Julius Caesar more than two thousand years ago.

While the amount stays the same, water does change location. The movement of water from place to place is called the *water cycle*. This is how it works:

The sun's heat *evaporates* (dries up) moisture from large bodies of water, particularly oceans. The water rises into the sky and forms clouds. When the clouds get heavy with moisture, rain or snow falls from them. The rain or snow lands on the ground and on the oceans. The heat of the sun dries up the moisture, starting the water cycle over again.

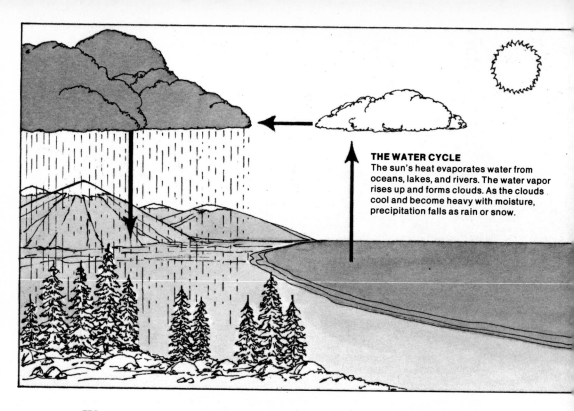

THE WATER CYCLE
The sun's heat evaporates water from oceans, lakes, and rivers. The water vapor rises up and forms clouds. As the clouds cool and become heavy with moisture, precipitation falls as rain or snow.

When there's a drought in a certain region, it doesn't mean that our planet has less water. It just means that this particular region isn't getting its usual share of moisture. At the same time, another area may be getting too much rain. The next year the situation could be reversed. The dry region could be flooded and the wet one could be struck by drought.

What Is a Drought?

A drought occurs when rainfall drops well below normal for a prolonged period of time in a given area. This doesn't mean that the area gets no rain. It means that not enough rain falls at the right time to support the life that's there.

If the soil is very dry to start with, the ground may still be parched despite any rain that falls. It's the same with small rainstorms during droughts. The ground may be so dry that it will take several inches of rain to replenish the moisture.

In some desert areas much of the seasonal rain may fall in one or two big rainstorms. Because the rain falls too fast, or at the wrong time, drought may continue in the area.

The bed of Swan Lake (above), a South Dakota waterfowl refuge, has been dry since 1974 because of drought conditions.

Droughts Can Occur Anywhere

Each kind of land has a normal amount of rainfall. Deserts get less than ten inches of rain per year. Jungles receive more than eighty inches in a normal year. Much of the Great Plains of the United States receives about twenty inches of moisture per year.

What is plentiful rainfall for one place may cause a drought in another. For example, five inches of rain in two months would be adequate for crops in the Great Plains. But it would cause a severe drought in a jungle. The jungle plants need much more rain to survive.

What is plentiful rainfall for one part of the earth may not be enough to prevent drought in another. Enough rain falls on the dry grasslands of the Serengeti Plain in Tanzania (above) to support abundant wildlife, but not enough to support farm crops. Very little vegetation can survive in the hot, dry climate of Coral Pink Sand Dunes State Park in Utah (below). Lack of sufficient rain in the Florida Everglades can cause the swamps to dry up (opposite top), but when rain is plentiful there, vegetation thrives (opposite bottom).

Very few plants can grow in Arizona's Painted Desert (above).

Cactus and other desert plants can go long periods without much water. But if a desert goes without rain long enough, even the hardy plants and animals there will die.

Droughts can occur anywhere. There have been droughts just about every place in the world.

What Causes Weather?

Will it be hot or cold tomorrow? Will it be dry or rainy, windy or calm? The daily changes in temperature, moisture, and wind are all part of what is called the *weather*. Drought is just one type of weather.

The sun is the main factor in causing all weather. The sun provides heat and light for our planet. If the sun were to disappear, the earth would have no weather. It would be a frozen, lifeless place.

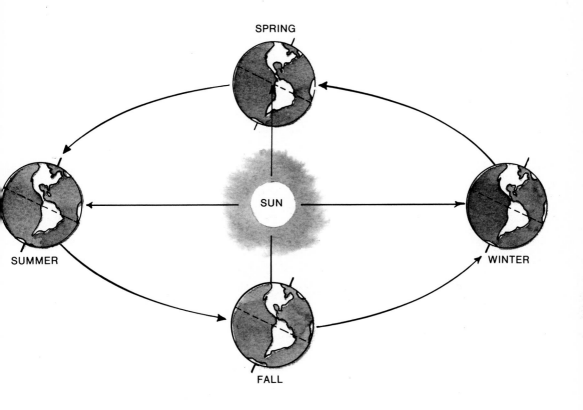

SPRING

SUN

SUMMER

WINTER

FALL

Northern Hemisphere seasons

The seasons are the most obvious example of the sun's influence on our weather. The earth orbits the sun in 365 ¼ days—one year. The seasons occur as the earth moves in its orbit, because the sun shines from different angles on a given location.

As we know, the sun evaporates ocean water that becomes rain and snow. But did you know that the sun also creates wind? Some parts of the earth receive more heat than other parts at a given time. In places that are hot, the air rises. In cold places the air sinks. The rising and falling movements of these large masses of air are felt as winds.

A windstorm sweeps over Mono Lake in central California near the Nevada border.

The earth's features also shape its weather. The oceans are a major influence, but land geography is also important. For example, flatlands don't do a good job of stopping the wind. That is why flatlands often experience summer windstorms and winter blizzards.

Once we know something about the causes of weather, we can begin to understand why droughts occur.

What Causes Droughts?

While scientists don't know what causes every drought, they are able to trace some droughts to interactions of the sun, wind, and oceans, or even to volcanic activity.

*If the monsoon winds (above) do not bring rain to
southern Asia during the summer, drought occurs.*

One type of drought is caused by the failure of the
monsoons. Monsoons are winds that help to create two distinct
seasons in India and the rest of southern Asia. In the winter,
the monsoons blow from the north and bring with them cool,
dry weather. The dry weather usually ends in the summer,
when the monsoons blow from the south. The monsoon
winds then pick up moisture from the Indian Ocean and dump
it as rain on southern Asia. The moisture is needed to grow
the crops that feed millions.

Sometimes during the summer monsoon season there are

strong west winds over the Indian Ocean. These winds push the moisture eastward. Because the rains fall over the Indian Ocean instead of on the land, a drought occurs.

Because oceans supply most of the moisture to make rain, they play a major role in creating droughts. The sun's heat evaporates large amounts of ocean water, creating rain clouds. There are years when certain oceans don't get as warm as usual. Less water evaporates into the air, and so some areas receive less than their normal amount of rain.

Volcanic eruptions can help cause droughts by sending huge amounts of dust high into the sky. The dust blocks out sunlight, causing our oceans to cool slightly. Cool air holds less moisture and brings less rain than warm air. It is also thought that air pollution, like volcanic dust, may contribute to drought by blocking out sunlight.

Meteorologists (weather scientists) have been studying global weather for only a few years. They continually gather more data so that the causes of droughts will be better understood. They are also studying our master weather control—the sun—to see if changes in it may be the ultimate cause of most droughts.

Drought Patterns and the Master Control: the Sun

There were no meteorologists to keep track of droughts that took place hundreds of years ago. Yet we have records of such droughts. These records can be found inside trees.

Each year of its life, a tree grows a new layer of wood. A tree that is one hundred years old will have one hundred layers. If the trunk of the tree is cut open, these layers can be seen as rings.

Scientists can discover drought patterns by studying the rings of very old trees.

In years of plentiful rainfall, trees grow thick rings. During dry spells, trees don't grow much, so their rings are thin. By studying the rings of very old trees, scientists can tell what a region's weather was like a hundred or even a thousand years ago.

Tree rings and other clues (including the study of ancient pollen) indicate that droughts may occur at regular intervals. For example, droughts seem to occur on America's Great Plains at twenty-two-year intervals. Droughts are thought to occur in Africa's Sahel region at about that same frequency. Droughts on the lower reaches of China's Yellow River occur every nine or ten years.

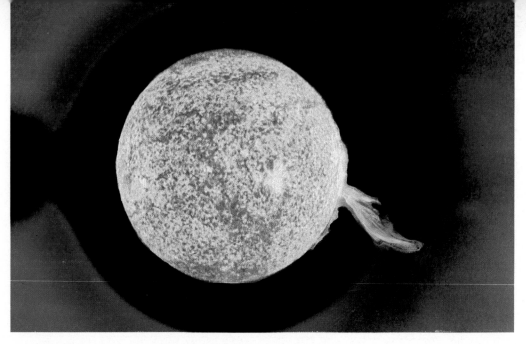

Some scientists believe that increases and decreases in the sun's energy (above) may affect our weather.

A number of scientists are studying the connection between periodic droughts and changes in the sun. They think droughts, as well as other weather variations, occur because the sun's energy increases and decreases in cycles. Scientists hope that by learning more about the sun's cycle, they can begin to predict when droughts are likely to occur. People could then be better prepared for long spells of dry weather.

How Droughts Harm the Land

Droughts leave scars on the land that take years to heal. When thousands of square miles of grass, trees, and shrubs are destroyed by a major drought, the land may not be green for many years—it can take an entire human lifetime for a new forest to grow.

Soil also becomes *eroded* (worn or moved away) during droughts, especially when there are dust storms. In most places, there are only ten inches of topsoil. Farmers plant

Wind erosion occurs when dust storms, such as this one in Cochran County, Texas, blow away the topsoil from farmland.

their crops in the topsoil, which is the upper layer of soil. It takes roughly a hundred years for each inch of topsoil to form. During a single dust storm, a farm can lose much of its topsoil—wrecking what it took nature a thousand years to create.

How Droughts Harm People

Hunger is the immediate problem for those involved in a drought. Without water, crops and cattle die. People are left with little or nothing to eat. When an area has widespread hunger, it is said to be suffering from *famine*. Although famine can take place for many other reasons—floods or war, for example—famines caused by droughts have been among the worst disasters ever to strike human beings.

These Peul nomads lost all their cattle during the Sahelian drought of the 1970s.

Although hunger is a great problem, disease is usually the main killer during famines. Weakened by hunger, people are much more susceptible to disease. A recent example of a drought-caused famine occurred in Africa's Sahel region during the 1970s. Disease killed 200,000 persons.

The poorer a country, the more vulnerable it is to famine. Poor nations don't have the money or transportation systems needed to get food to their people quickly. They often lack television or radio, so they cannot warn people about a famine's dangers.

Lack of clean water is another killer during droughts. As rivers, ponds, and wells dry up, people and livestock have nothing to drink. They may drink contaminated water, which can lead to disease and death.

The dust storms that accompany droughts are deadly, too. People and animals choke to death. The survivors may suffer from breathing problems years after inhaling the dust.

Because the midwestern drought of 1871 dried out the wooden buildings of Chicago, Illinois, a small fire turned into a major conflagration that destroyed much of the city (above).

Droughts also can cause fires. In 1871, drought dried out the midwestern United States. By early fall, there were small fires in the forests and swamps of northern Wisconsin. Because of the extreme dryness, these fires started by themselves through the process of spontaneous combustion. On October 8, 1871, fire killed approximately fifteen hundred persons in and around Peshtigo, Wisconsin. The wooden buildings of Chicago, Illinois also were dried out by the drought. On the same day as the Peshtigo Fire—October 8, 1871—a terrible fire destroyed much of Chicago and killed at least three hundred persons. Few people realize that drought was a major factor in both the Peshtigo Fire and the Great Chicago Fire.

Because droughts last longer than other natural disasters, they create an especially great hardship for people. As they wait day after day for rain, people feel more and more helpless and depressed. They worry about when the drought will end and what they will eat if the crops don't grow.

The Cliff Dwellers who built homes in the mountains of Colorado (above) may have died out because of the droughts that occurred between 1250 and 1300.

4/SOME DEADLY DROUGHTS

Because they create famines, droughts have been among the deadliest of all natural disasters. Drought-caused famines have killed millions of persons in a single year.

Civilizations have been ended by droughts. About 2500 B.C., one of the world's first great civilizations emerged in the Indus River Valley. Its two main cities were Harappa and Mohenjo-daro, both located in what is now Pakistan. In about 1700 B.C., this civilization faded. Many scientists blame droughts.

A thousand years ago, Indians (including the Cliff Dwellers) flourished in what is now the southwestern United States. But around the year 1300, their civilization dwindled and disappeared. Droughts were probably a major cause. Tree ring studies indicate that the Southwest suffered severe droughts between 1250 and 1300.

Although droughts and famines have killed millions and ended civilizations, little is known about many of the deadliest ones. That is because they occurred in nations where few written records were kept. Furthermore, many of the worst famines have occurred in remote regions. Often, outsiders didn't even know of the disasters until many persons had died.

China's Drought of the 1870s

China's Yellow River Valley was one of the four areas where civilization began. The other three "cradles of civilization" were the Indus Valley in Pakistan, the Nile

Valley in Egypt, and the Tigris-Euphrates Valley in the Middle East.

Today—four thousand years after civilization developed there—China is the most populous nation on earth. It is also the world's third largest country.

Because of its large population and its geography, China has suffered more from natural disasters than any other nation. Of China's numerous earthquakes, the one that killed 830,000 persons in 1556 was the deadliest ever to rock our planet. China's many floods have drowned people and caused famines by wrecking crops. The 1887 Yellow River flood and subsequent famine killed up to 6 million persons. These figures are staggering, yet China's hundreds of droughts have probably claimed more lives than all the country's earthquakes and floods combined.

From 1876 to 1879, little rain fell on northern China. Wheat, sorghum, and millet dried up in a 300,000-square-mile region. Many millions of persons were left with little or nothing to eat.

It was difficult for the Chinese government to determine which areas needed food the most. It was even more of a problem to transport the food. Piles of food were collected in the port city of Tientsin. The food was put on carts and wagons but much of it never reached the villages. The supply

In 1877, drought in China caused such severe famine that many families were forced to sell their children to be able to buy bread.

wagons were attacked by desperate people. Even the camels, oxen, and donkeys that pulled the wagons were killed and eaten by starving people.

As the drought continued, roads and fields filled with starving people. Although many died of hunger, others were killed by hungry wolves, foxes, and dogs. As is usual during droughts, many people weakened and died of disease. In places where food was available, people killed each other fighting for it.

It is not known exactly how many died during China's drought and famine of 1876-79. Most experts place the death toll at 9 to 13 million, making this one of the worst disasters ever to strike human beings.

Droughts in India

Like China, India depends on the summer monsoons to bring rain. When the monsoons fail, drought occurs. India is a poor nation. Even in normal times, many of its people go hungry.

India suffered a horrendous drought in 1769-70. Millions of persons wandered about in search of food. It is thought that up to 10 million perished during these two years, many from the disease called *smallpox.*

Among India's many other droughts was the terrible drought of 1865-66. Again, up to 10 million lives were lost.

There was enough food in India to feed people during the drought of the 1860s. But the English, who ruled India at the time, decided that grain should be sold rather than given to the poor. Wealthy Indian merchants also hoarded grain and then sold it at high prices to the few who could pay. In 1867, when the government finally decided to send rice into the afflicted areas, monsoon rains wrecked roads. The supply carts couldn't get through.

The English did make some effort to combat droughts in India. They built irrigation projects to bring water to dry lands. They also helped formulate India's *Famine Code*, a plan to detect food shortages and then distribute food to the needy.

Two Russian Droughts

The Winter of 1890-91 was very cold in Russia, but snowfall was light. The snowmelt in the spring of 1891 provided little water for farm fields, and the weather was very dry. Western Russia experienced a drought. Ponds and wells dried up and winds lifted topsoil high into the sky. The grain harvest—particularly of rye, which was the main food source for many peasants—was poor.

Russia did have a system to combat famine. During years of plentiful harvests, farmers were supposed to fill storehouses with grain so that there would be enough food during famine years. In addition, Russia's government had a plan to distribute money, food, and seeds during famines.

While this system was a good idea, it didn't work well. The farmers were too poor to keep the storehouses filled. Russia's government didn't have nearly enough money or grain to combat a major famine. Geography also presented a big problem. Russia is the world's largest country, and during the 1890s, it lacked a transportation system that could distribute food throughout a wide area.

Trains on the few rail lines were loaded with grain. But

During a drought and famine in the late 1800s, these starving Russian villagers on their way to get relief spent a night in a farm stable.

during the winter of 1891-92, snowdrifts blocked tracks. Another problem was the lack of water to make steam for the locomotives. (In some cases, snow was gathered from along the tracks and then heated. Once the snow turned into water, the stalled locomotives could move.)

When the United States and European nations heard about the famine, they sent food to Russia. Their efforts saved many lives. But each day, thousands more died. As in most famines, hunger wasn't the main killer. Of the 400,000 persons who died in this famine, most probably succumbed to illness.

Thirty years later, in 1921-22, Russia's Volga River basin was stricken by a horrible famine. Russia's grain supply had been depleted during World War I and the Civil War of 1918-20. To make matters worse, a drought in 1921 had turned fields into blackened deserts. By 1922, 30 million people in an area of a million square miles were suffering from famine.

The Russian government and relief agencies from other nations tried to help. The American Relief Administration provided food for millions of persons. Yet millions of others went hungry. A member of the religious group called the Quakers described the famine: "I saw in practically every home benches covered with birch or lime leaves. These are dried, pounded, mixed with acorns, some dirt and water, and then baked into a substance which they call bread. . . . The children cannot digest this food and they die. . . . According to Government figures, 90 percent of the children between the ages of one and three have already died from the famine."

It is estimated that up to 5 million persons died in the Russian famine of 1921-22. This was more people than Russia lost during World War I, which had ended a few years earlier.

Africa's Sahel Drought of the 1970s

The Sahel is a large region of Africa. It lies south of the Sahara Desert, and is made up of parts of six countries: Mauritania, Senegal, Mali, Upper Volta, Niger, and Chad.

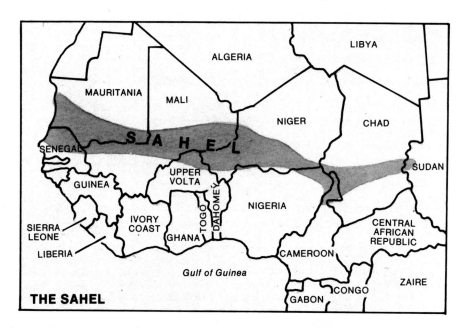

THE SAHEL

At one time these countries were colonies of France. Upon gaining complete independence in 1960, the new nations hoped to improve life for their people.

Even during the best of times, life has been hard for those in the Sahel. It is a very dry region, averaging between four and twelve inches of rain yearly. Partly because of frequent droughts, hunger has always been a problem.

During their first few years of independence, however, the new nations seemed to have nature on their side. During much of the 1960s, the region had adequate rainfall. This was good for the farmers, who grew peanuts and sorghum. It also helped the herders, who raised cattle, sheep, camels, and goats. The herders were *nomads*—they traveled with their animals in search of grassland and water.

But in the late 1960s, drought struck the Sahel. The region had experienced many droughts before, so at first people weren't especially alarmed. But gradually they realized that this drought was different from others—it went on year after year until the mid-1970s.

As fields dried out, crops died. In a desperate effort to survive, many people ate seeds that had been saved for the next planting. By eating the seeds, they were left with nothing to plant. But when human beings are suffering from hunger, they don't always think of the future.

As available grass was eaten, livestock died. The animals could be seen lying on sun-scorched fields and next to dried-up rivers. According to some estimates, more than 30 million animals died in 1973 alone.

Many persons were kept alive only because dead cattle were eaten. Weakened by hunger, thousands of others died of disease.

By summer of 1973, the governments of the Sahelian

countries realized the seriousness of the situation. But communication in these countries was poor. By the time the rest of the world knew about the famine, a disaster of huge proportions had already occurred.

Rivers dried up into muddy streams. Thirst-crazed elephants stampeded in search of water. People were so distraught at seeing their loved ones suffering that they wandered out into the desert to die. This was the situation that the United Nations and other organizations found when they sent representatives into Africa's Sahel in 1973.

Relief work was difficult. The people were spread out over a huge area. The amount of food and supplies required was immense.

The United Nations and individual countries donated millions of tons of food to the people of the Sahel. Medicines were sent in for the sick. Seeds and farm supplies for future plantings were provided. These materials were sent in by boat and airplane, train and truck, camel and donkey caravan.

Between 50,000 and 200,000 persons perished in the Sahel drought of the early 1970s. Without these relief efforts, millions might have died.

What is the future of the Sahel and its people? Some *climatologists* (scientists who study our planet's past weather) say that the Sahel is undergoing a long-term climatic change. They point out that droughts during the past fifty years have turned approximately 250,000 square miles of the Sahel into desert. Meanwhile, the great Sahara Desert seems to be creeping southward at a pace of thirty miles per year in some places. Scientists say that extremely dry weather will be normal for the Sahel, and that it is useless to attempt to farm or raise livestock in the region.

Other scientists disagree, however. They say that the Sahel

Top: These Upper Volta tribesmen, victims of the catastrophic five-year-long drought and famine in the Sahel region of Africa, had watched their herds of cattle vanish from starvation as pastures turned into wastelands.
Bottom: This starving Peul tribeswoman sat in front of a food-distribution center in Niger as she waited for the daily ration of sorghum supplied by the Food and Agricultural Organization of the United Nations.

merely experienced a very bad drought, and that conditions were made worse because livestock had overgrazed the pasture. Those who think that the Sahel can be saved propose building irrigation projects to help the people who live there.

It will take years to determine whether or not the Sahel is undergoing a permanent change in climate. In the meantime, millions face future droughts as they try to farm and herd livestock in this region of Africa.

SOME MAJOR DROUGHTS

Date	Place	Approximate Number of Deaths
1064-72	Egypt	Unknown
1333-37	China	Possibly more than 4 million
1630	India	Many thousands
1769-70	India	Estimated at between 3 and 10 million
1790-92	India	Called the "Skull Famine" because skulls filled the countryside, this disaster killed unknown thousands
1803-04	India	Thousands
1837-38	India	800,000
1865-66	India	Possibly 10 million
1868-70	India	Many thousands
1876-78	India	In the province of Madras alone, 3.5 million persons died
1876-79	China	Estimated at between 9 and 13 million
1891-92	Russia	400,000
1892-94	China	Nearly a million
1896-97	India	Estimated at 5 million
1899-1900	India	More than 1 million
1920-21	China	500,000
1921-22	Russia	Up to 5 million
1930s	Midwestern United States	Unknown, but extremely low compared to the death tolls during droughts in other countries
1932-33	The Ukraine	5 million
1972-74	The Sahel nations of Africa	Between 50,000 and 200,000
1973-74	Ethiopia	100,000

5/SAVING PEOPLE FROM DROUGHT AND FAMINE

Throughout much of history, people have been helpless against drought and famine. In addition, nations have warred and argued with each other so much that it has been difficult to coordinate relief efforts.

In this century, these problems have been at least partly solved. Better communication and transportation systems speed relief efforts. People also have formed organizations to help hungry nations.

Bringing Food to Needy Areas

Bihar is a state in northeastern India with more than 56 million people. Bihar has experienced many famines. A terrible drought in 1769-70 killed up to 10 million persons in Bihar and nearby areas.

In the mid-1960s Bihar and neighboring regions were again stricken by drought. Indira Gandhi, prime minister of India, said: "Countless millions of our people. . . have had the bread taken out of their mouths by an abnormal failure of the rains. . . . The grain has died on the stalk. The toil and sweat of months have been reduced to dust. There is hunger and distress in millions of homes."

In the past, a drought like this could have claimed millions of lives. But in the 1960s, word of the Bihar drought quickly spread around the world. Nations responded by sending food and other aid.

*Above: China's Red Flag Canal near Anyang brings water to
thirsty farmland.*
*Below: Roosevelt Dam on the Salt River in south-central Arizona
is used for irrigation, flood control, and power production.*

The United States provided the most relief. It sent 9 million tons of wheat to India. Day after day, shiploads of wheat and other foods arrived in India. The food was sent by truck and train to needy areas. As a result, famine was averted.

Individual nations and charitable organizations often help when famines threaten today. There is also a worldwide organization that works for world peace and a better quality of life for all people. It is called the United Nations (UN). The UN keeps food supplies ready for times of possible famine. The UN also maintains a warning system to inform the world about famine situations.

Despite modern efforts, famines still create massive disasters. The Sahel famine of the 1970s killed thousands before relief efforts swung into action. Yet without the help that eventually came from the UN and individual countries, the Sahel famine could have killed many, many more.

Fighting Droughts

One way to fight the effects of drought is with *irrigation.* Irrigation means bringing water to farmlands by artificial means. Irrigation is not used only for drought conditions. It also can turn land that is always dry into land suitable for crops. Millions of acres around the world are receiving water through irrigation systems.

Dam Irrigation: One method to provide water to irrigate fields is to build dams on nearby rivers. The dam's block the rivers and store the water in artificial lakes called reservoirs. The water is then sent through ditches and canals to thirsty farmland.

The United States has thousands of irrigation dams. The Colorado River, which flows 1,450 miles through the southwestern United States and part of Mexico, provides huge amounts of irrigation water. The famous Hoover Dam and other dams block off the water of the Colorado. The water is stored in big reservoirs. It is then sent through canals to dry farmland in an area that includes parts of Arizona, Nevada, California, and Mexico. After providing water for its last irrigation project in Mexico, the Colorado River is just a tiny stream. Most of its water has been diverted in irrigation projects along the way.

Dams have other functions besides helping with irrigation. They assist in flood control. They also can be used to convert waterpower into electricity. In China—a nation often stricken by floods and droughts—dams are used for all three purposes. They generate electricity, control floods by blocking off water, and store irrigation water in reservoirs. There are many dams and reservoirs on China's rivers, particularly along the Yellow and Yangtze rivers. Although China has had droughts in recent years, the country's irrigation projects have helped prevent large-scale famines.

Russia, India, Australia, Thailand, and Egypt are five other countries that make extensive use of dams and reservoirs for irrigation. Egypt's Aswan High Dam was completed in 1970. During Egypt's rainy season in August, the dam holds back the high waters of the Nile River. The water is stored in Lake Nasser. During dry periods, water from this artificial lake is used to irrigate parched farmlands.

Groundwater Irrigation: River water floats on the earth's surface. But beneath the surface, there is another source of water—groundwater.

Groundwater is stored in spaces between underground

rocks. Some of the water comes from rain and snow that trickles down below the earth's surface.

Groundwater is a bigger source of water than all of the earth's rivers and lakes combined. In fact, there is thirty times as much fresh water under the ground as there is in all the earth's rivers and lakes.

Large pools of groundwater are called *aquifers.* One huge aquifer in the United States is called the Ogallala Aquifer. It stretches for eight hundred miles between South Dakota and Texas and contains enough water to fill Lake Huron.

Wells are used in the United States and around the world to tap groundwater for drinking and for irrigation. However there's only a certain amount of groundwater. It can take thousands of years to fill an underground aquifer. In some places in the United States and other countries, people are pumping up groundwater faster than nature is replacing it. This means that wells have to be sunk deeper and deeper to reach the groundwater. Scientists fear that one day all the groundwater in certain regions will be used up.

Other Irrigation Methods: Rivers and groundwater are the two main sources for irrigation; but people have thought of other methods to obtain irrigation water. Dew collecting, rain collecting, and the condensation of seawater are some unusual irrigation methods used in various places of the world.

Perhaps the most interesting and controversial irrigation method is *rainmaking,* also known as *cloud seeding.* Rain falls from clouds when the water gets so heavy that the clouds can't hold it. In the United States, scientists have used airplanes to drop chemicals into clouds. The chemicals help make the water droplets heavy enough to fall as rain.

Rainmaking has worked in the United States, but scientists,

farmers, and lawmakers have long argued about it. Some say that this method works only when the clouds are about ready to drop their rain anyway. Farmers worry that when rain is made to fall in one place, another region may suffer from drought.

Rainmaking is now banned in some parts of the United States. Experiments are being conducted in the western states to provide answers. If these problems can be solved, cloud seeding may again become a practical way to produce rain in drought-stricken regions.

Improved Farming Methods

In recent years, many nations have developed improved farming methods to help people survive droughts.

Contour plowing became popular after America's Dust Bowl era. Fields that have been contour plowed can retain rain better because furrows are made *across,* rather than *up* slopes.

In the United States, many farmers allow parts of their fields to lie *fallow* (idle) each year. Because there are no crops to use the water, soil moisture builds up in the ground during the year. Moisture is then available when crops are planted the following year.

To prevent soil erosion and dust storms, many farmers plant *cover crops.* These crops enrich the soil and help hold it down. In other efforts to combat soil erosion and dust storms, the United States has made laws to preserve the native vegetation on national lands.

Improved seeds are another help to farmers. Scientists have developed seeds that require less moisture than those of the past, while producing larger and faster-growing crops.

Strip cropping (above), contour plowing (left), and terracing (below) are three farming methods that help conserve soil.

To help reclaim the land lost during the dust storms of the 1930s, the Soil Conservation Service initiated programs to help farmers irrigate their land and prevent future wind erosion and water erosion. This alfalfa field in Oklahoma, irrigated by water from a nearby reservoir, produced a bumper crop in 1940.

When these methods of preventing drought were first introduced, they were not always accepted by the people who made their living from the land. It is natural for herders to want the largest herds possible, and for farmers to want to plant crops on all available land. Big crops and large herds make more money. But experts remind us that overgrazing the grasslands and digging up too much farmland can lead to more disasters like those that crippled the Dust Bowl and the African Sahel.

Woolly mammoths at the edge of a Pleistocene Ice Age glacier

Is the Earth Cooling?

Climate is the word used to describe the kind of weather an area has over many years. Climate changes. Periodically, the earth has undergone cold periods called *ice ages*. There have been prolonged dry periods, as well as times when large portions of land were covered by water. The place where you live may have been covered by swamps at one time and by ice at another.

About one and three-quarters million years ago, thick ice covered much of North America, Europe, and Asia. This ice age lasted until about ten thousand years ago. Later, from 1550 to 1850, the earth experienced a prolonged period of

Death Valley, California (above) and Sand Dunes National Monument in Colorado (below) are desert areas that experience constant drought.

Some areas of the world, such as China (above) and parts of California
experience periodic droughts. The level of Lake Berryessa in
Napa County, California, receded drastically during the 1977 drought (below).

The world's population, already nearly five billion, is expected to double by the year 2025. In the meantime, we will have to find ways to produce enough food to support our hungry world.

cold weather—a "little ice age." Then, from about 1850 to about 1950, the climate grew warmer.

Scientists have evidence that the global climate has cooled since about 1950. Some think we may be entering another "little ice age." While this doesn't mean that our cities will be covered by snow in July, it does mean that we may expect slightly lower year-round temperatures. The effects of colder weather are usually droughts, midsummer frosts, and other unstable weather patterns. To be prepared for these problems, we need to learn all we can about droughts and how we can best help the people who are hit hardest by them.

The Problem of World Hunger

Today there are half a billion people on earth who either don't get enough food or can't obtain the kinds of foods needed by the human body. The human population is expected to double by the year 2025. Yet many scientists feel that, even with several times its current population, the earth could feed every living person.

You've already read about the modern farming and irrigation methods used to combat drought. Scientists also are working to tap new food sources. Many speak of "farming the sea" in the future. There are many edible animals and plants in the sea that are currently unused. In the future, seaweeds, sea grasses, and many sea animals may become food for people.

Scientists have many other ideas for producing food for a hungry world. We may not be able to prevent droughts in the future, but if people learn to work together, we ought to be able to prevent the hunger and disease that are the worst effects of drought.

Cape Cod sand dunes

Glossary

Aquifer   A large pool of groundwater

Black blizzard   A dust storm that blots out the sunlight

Climatologist   A scientist who studies our planet's past weather

Cloud seeding (rainmaking)   The process of dropping chemicals into clouds to make rain fall

Contour plowing   A method of plowing furrows across slopes, rather than up and down slopes, to help prevent soil erosion

Drought   A prolonged period when rainfall is well below normal in a given area

Dust bowl   The region of the United States (including parts of Kansas, Colorado, New Mexico, Texas, and Oklahoma) that suffered the worst droughts and dust storms of the 1930s

Dust storm   A whirlwind carrying tons of loose dirt and sand that can move over hundreds of square miles of land; usually associated with hot dry air in regions where there has been soil erosion

Famine   A long period of widespread hunger that causes starvation and death, often caused by droughts

Groundwater   Water stored beneath the surface of the earth

Irrigation   Supplying water to farmland by artificial means

Meteorologist   A weather scientist

Monsoon   A periodic wind over the Indian Ocean that helps create two distinct seasons in southern Asia

Sod   Grass-covered ground

Sodbuster   A person who breaks up sod

Soil erosion   The wearing away of soil caused by the action of rain, running water, wind, ice, or temperature changes

Strip cropping   A method of planting strips of one kind of crop between strips of another kind of crop to help prevent soil erosion

Terracing   A method of farming on hillsides to prevent soil erosion by building wide, flat plateaus that resemble stair steps

Topsoil   The upper layer of fertile soil, usually about ten inches deep, in which farmers plant their crops

Water cycle   The circulation of water from the oceans to the air to the land and back to the oceans

Index
Page numbers in boldface type indicate illustrations

Photo Credits

About the Author

Dennis Fradin attended Northwestern University on a partial creative writing scholarship and graduated in 1967. He has published stories and articles in such places as *Ingenue, The Saturday Evening Post, Scholastic, Chicago, Oui,* and *National Humane Review.* His previous books include the Young People's Stories of Our States series for Childrens Press and *Bad Luck Tony* for Prentice-Hall. He is married and the father of three children.

About the Artist

Len Meents studied painting and drawing at Southern Illinois University and after graduation in 1969 he moved to Chicago. Mr. Meents works full time as a painter and illustrator. He and his wife and their two children currently make their home in LaGrange, Illinois.